welcome!

This Daily Prayer Journal is designed to deepen children's relationship with the Lord as they contemplate God, Gratitude and Scripture.

It is excellent as both a Prayer Journal, and for kids to intentionally practice creating a positive outlook on the rock of God's guidance each day.

We have designed it into A.M. / P.M. sections and have also included a prompts ideas page for your convenience (daily prompts may be customized as desired). There is an additional notes section at the end of the journal for extra space if needed.

Several pages have 'color me in' options, so your child may customize their prayer journal as desired.

It is a great idea to keep this book as a keepsake to track your child's prayers and progress, and watch how God moves in their life!

It is our prayer that your family's prayers are answered, and the love of God forever grows in your home.

With love and blessings,

Christian Scripture Journals

Some Prompts Suggestions:

Thankful for my mom/dad

Thankful for my sibling/s

Thankful for Jesus/God

Thankful for my friends

Thankful for my ability to
... problem solve,
stay positive, be thankful

Thankful for my teacher

Thankful for people's kindness
Thankful that I can help others

Thankful for the sun, moon and the stars

Thankful for my pet
Thankful for my home
Thankful for my good health

Thankful for other family members
(aunts, uncles, grandparents)

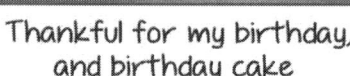

Thankful for my birthday, and birthday cake

Thankful for Christmas time (or other special holidays)

Thankful for fun and laughter

Thankful for spaghetti and meatballs
(or any other favorite foods)

Thankful for fun activities like travel, sports, camping

Thankful for the things I'm good at

Thankful for being me

The Lord's Prayer

Our Father, who art in heaven,
hallowed be Thy Name.
Thy Kingdom come,
Thy will be done
on Earth as it is in heaven.

Give us this day our daily bread.
And forgive us our trespasses,
as we forgive those who trespass
against us.

And lead us not into temptation,
but deliver us from evil.

For Thine is the Kingdom,
and the Power, and the Glory,
for ever and ever. Amen.

Date: S   M   T   W   TH   F   S   _____/_____/_____

Dear God, I love you and want you to know

Today will be a great day because

Today I am grateful for

A Bible Verse or something positive I will reflect on today is

I feel   very grumpy   grumpy   OK neutral   happy   very happy

because

Jesus Loves Me

Dear God, I love you and want you to know

Something I did well today was

Something important I learned today was

The best part of my day today was

My evening prayer: Tonight I pray

For others, I pray

Final thoughts (Example: forgiveness, special mention, requests)

Date: S M T W TH F S _____/_____/_____

Dear God, I love you and want you to know

Today will be a great day because

Today I am grateful for

A Bible Verse or something positive I will reflect on today is

I feel

very grumpy   grumpy   OK neutral   happy   very happy

because

Jesus Loves Me

Dear God, I love you and want you to know

Something I did well today was

Something important I learned today was

The best part of my day today was

My evening prayer: Tonight I pray

For others, I pray

Final thoughts (Example: forgiveness, special mention, requests)

Date: S   M   T   W   TH   F   S   _____/_____/_____

Dear God, I love you and want you to know

Today will be a great day because

Today I am grateful for

A Bible Verse or something positive I will reflect on today is

I feel   very grumpy   grumpy   OK neutral   happy   very happy

because

Jesus Loves Me

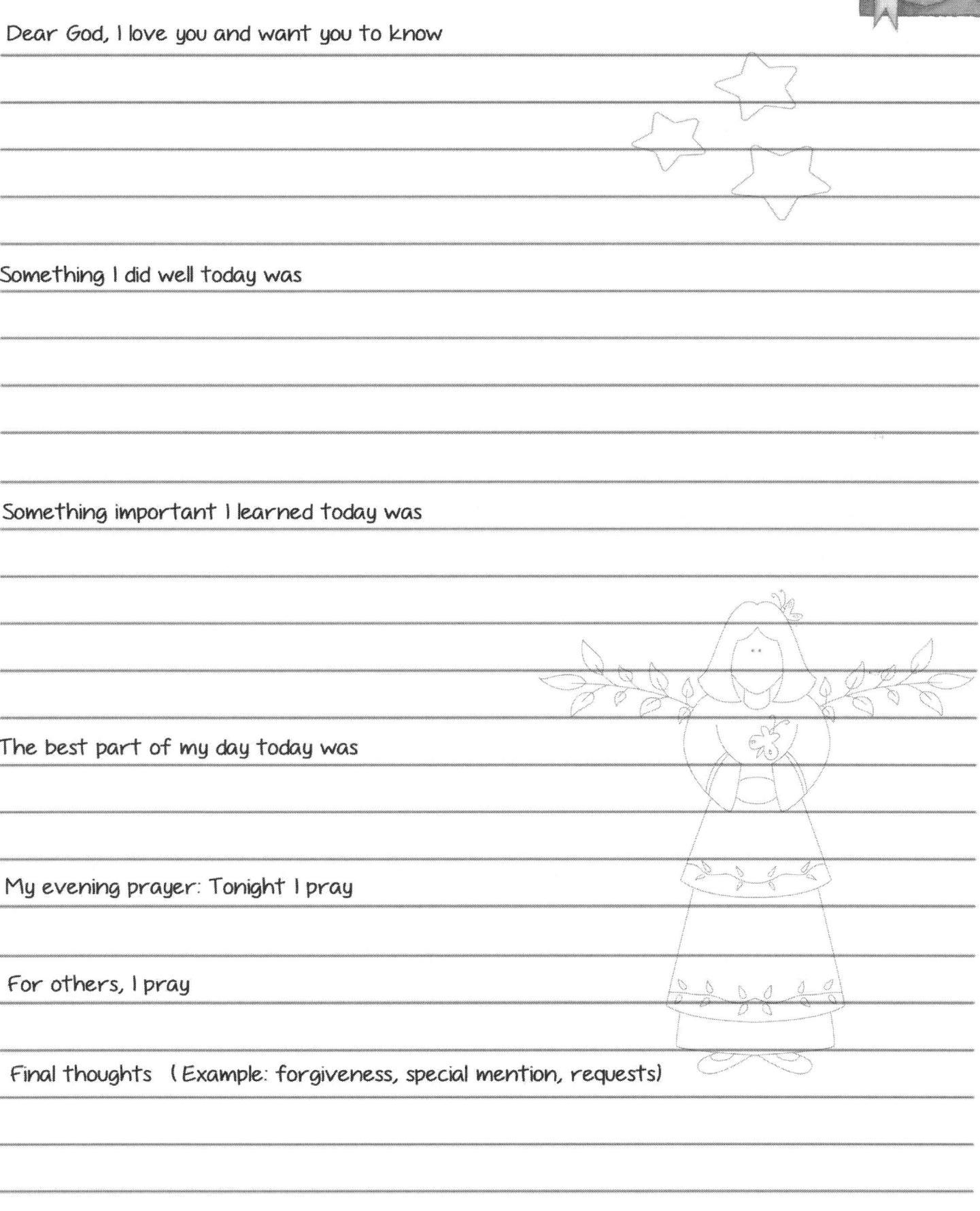

Dear God, I love you and want you to know

Something I did well today was

Something important I learned today was

The best part of my day today was

My evening prayer: Tonight I pray

For others, I pray

Final thoughts (Example: forgiveness, special mention, requests)

Date: S   M   T   W   TH   F   S   _____/_____/_____

Dear God, I love you and want you to know

Today will be a great day because

Today I am grateful for

A Bible Verse or something positive I will reflect on today is

I feel

because

very grumpy   grumpy   OK neutral   happy   very happy

Jesus Loves Me

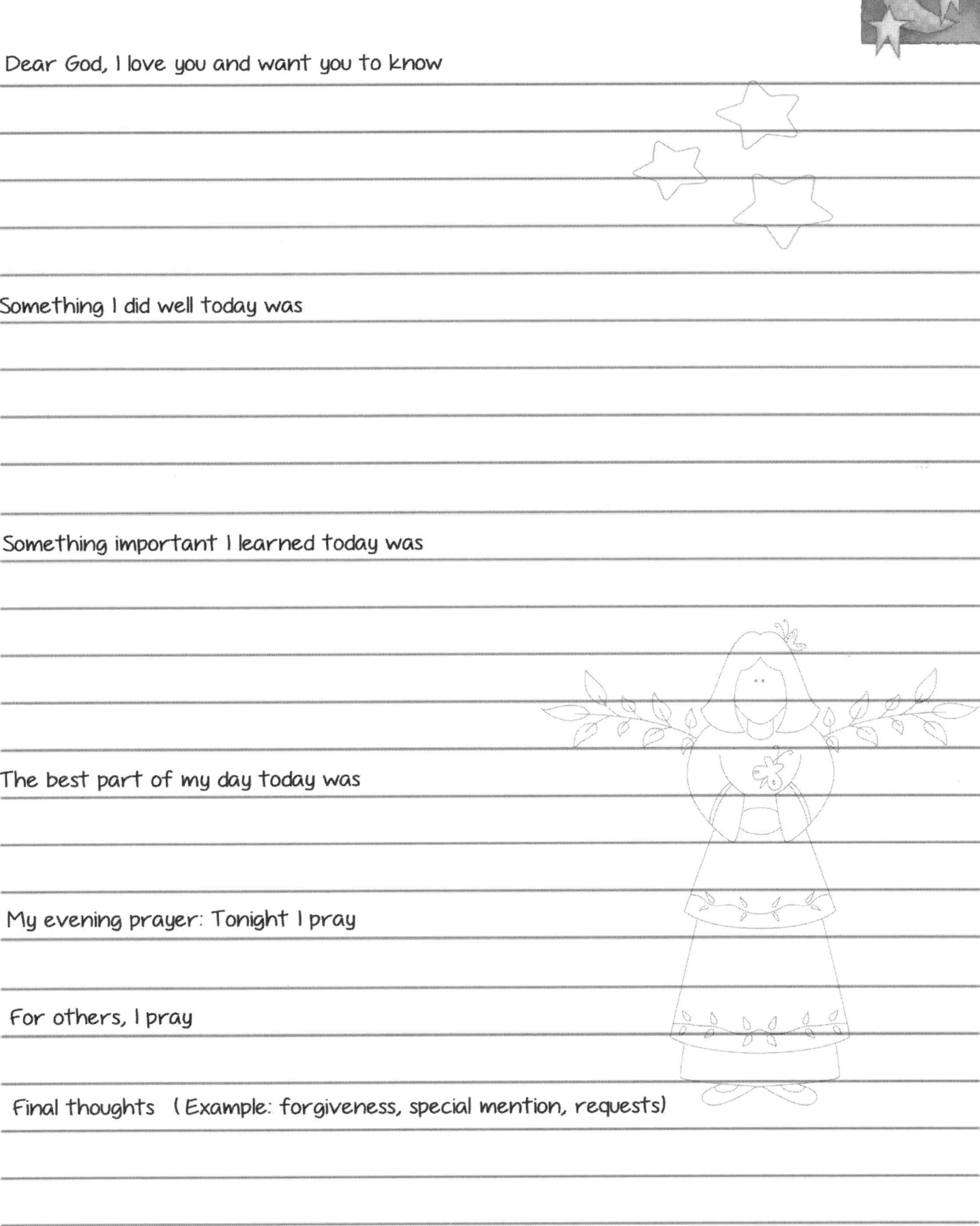

Dear God, I love you and want you to know

Something I did well today was

Something important I learned today was

The best part of my day today was

My evening prayer: Tonight I pray

For others, I pray

Final thoughts   (Example: forgiveness, special mention, requests)

Date: S M T W TH F S _____/_____/_____

Dear God, I love you and want you to know

Today will be a great day because

Today I am grateful for

A Bible Verse or something positive I will reflect on today is

I feel

very grumpy   grumpy   OK neutral   happy   very happy

because

Jesus Loves Me

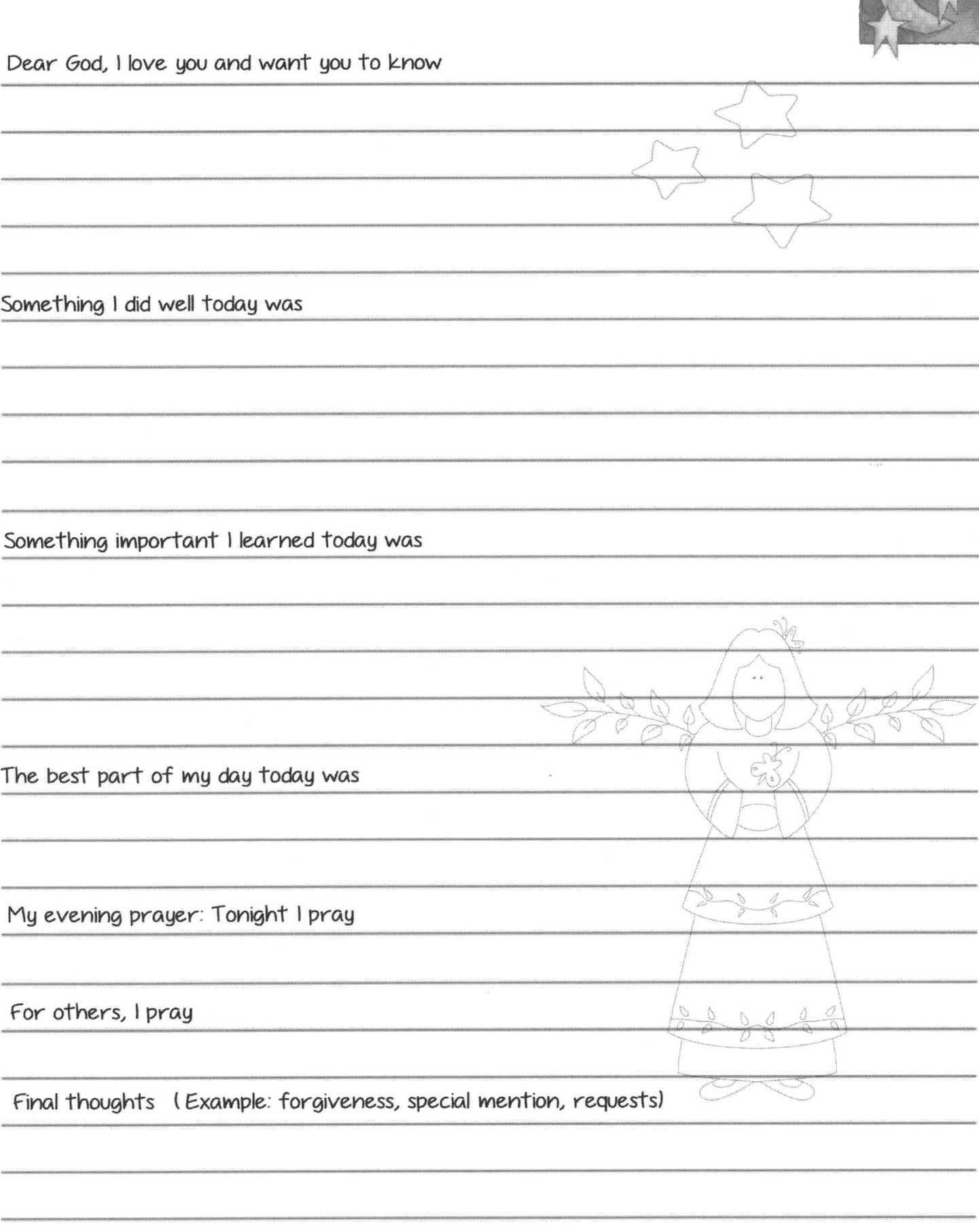

Dear God, I love you and want you to know

Something I did well today was

Something important I learned today was

The best part of my day today was

My evening prayer: Tonight I pray

For others, I pray

Final thoughts (Example: forgiveness, special mention, requests)

Date: S   M   T   W   TH   F   S   _____/_____/_____

Dear God, I love you and want you to know

Today will be a great day because

Today I am grateful for

A Bible Verse or something positive I will reflect on today is

I feel   very grumpy   grumpy   OK neutral   happy   very happy

because

Jesus Loves Me

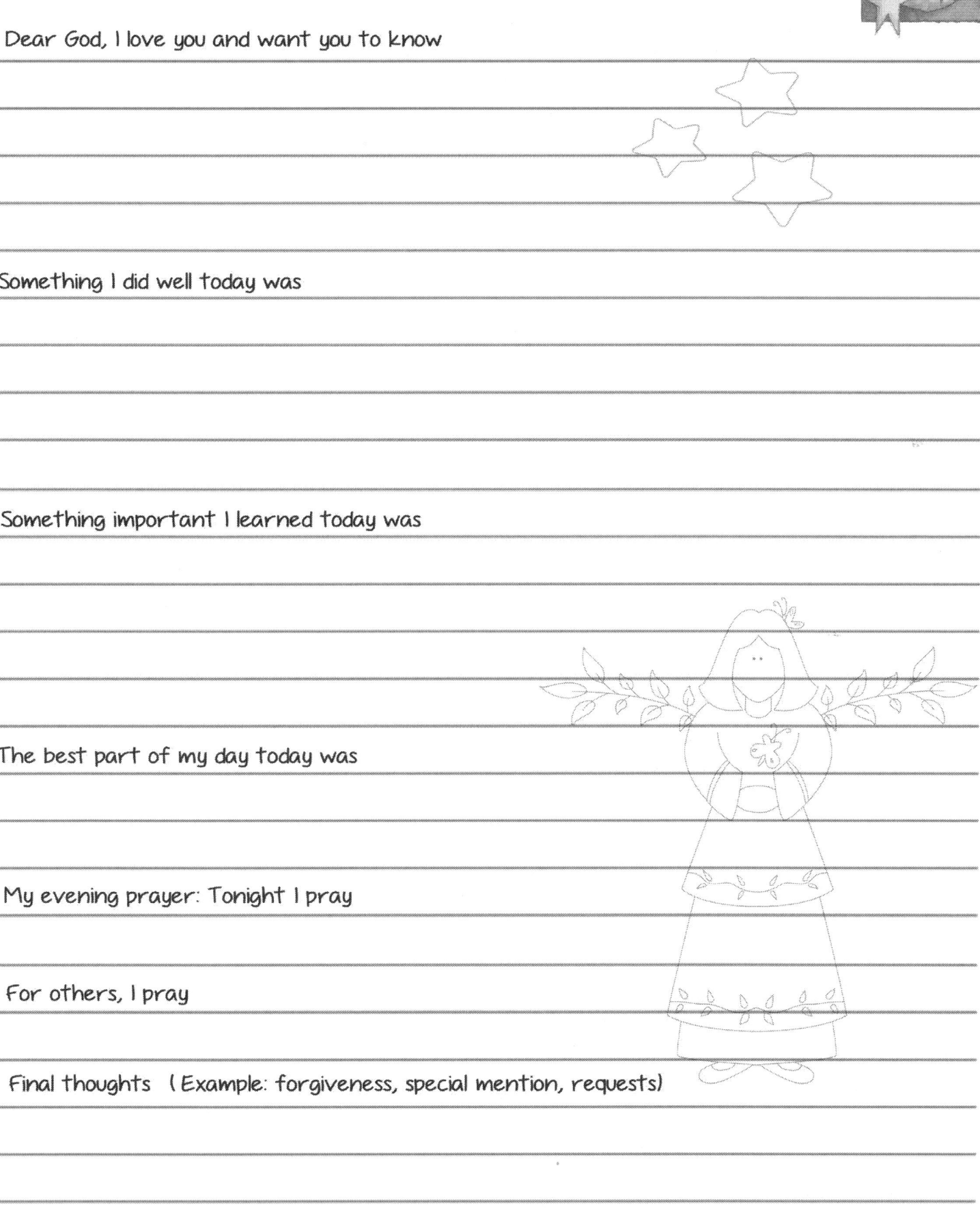

Dear God, I love you and want you to know

Something I did well today was

Something important I learned today was

The best part of my day today was

My evening prayer: Tonight I pray

For others, I pray

Final thoughts (Example: forgiveness, special mention, requests)

Date: S   M   T   W   TH   F   S   _____/_____/_____

Dear God, I love you and want you to know
_____
_____
_____
_____

Today will be a great day because
_____
_____
_____
_____
_____

Today I am grateful for
_____
_____
_____
_____
_____

A Bible Verse or something positive I will reflect on today is
_____
_____
_____

I feel   very grumpy   grumpy   OK neutral   happy   very happy

because
_____
_____
_____

Jesus Loves Me

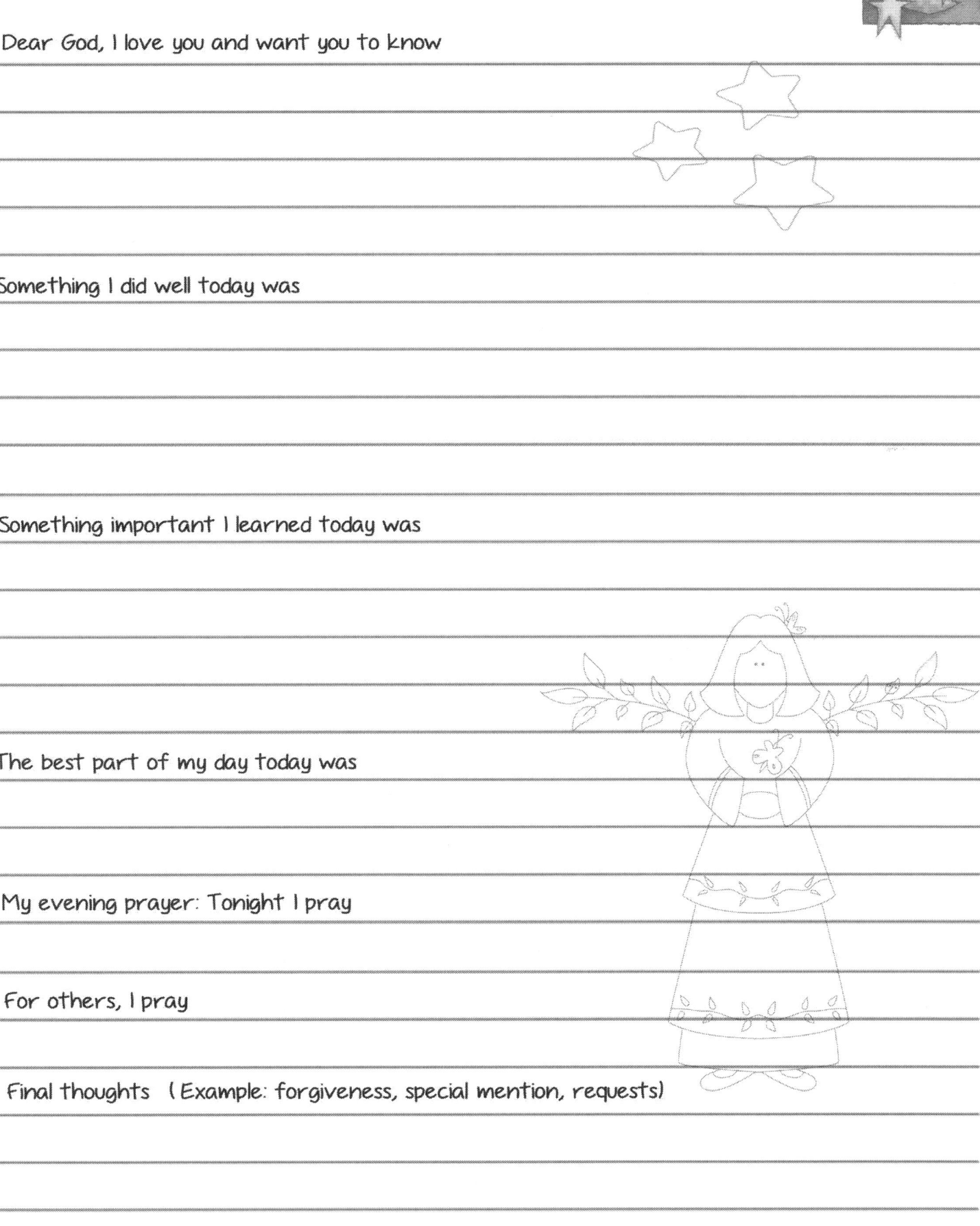

Dear God, I love you and want you to know

Something I did well today was

Something important I learned today was

The best part of my day today was

My evening prayer: Tonight I pray

For others, I pray

Final thoughts   (Example: forgiveness, special mention, requests)

Date: S   M   T   W   TH   F   S   _____/_____/_____

Dear God, I love you and want you to know
_____
_____
_____

Today will be a great day because
_____
_____
_____
_____

Today I am grateful for
_____
_____
_____
_____

A Bible Verse or something positive I will reflect on today is
_____
_____
_____

I feel   very grumpy   grumpy   OK neutral   happy   very happy

because
_____
_____
_____

Jesus Loves Me

Dear God, I love you and want you to know

Something I did well today was

Something important I learned today was

The best part of my day today was

My evening prayer: Tonight I pray

For others, I pray

Final thoughts (Example: forgiveness, special mention, requests)

Date: S   M   T   W   TH   F   S   _____/_____/_____

Dear God, I love you and want you to know

Today will be a great day because

Today I am grateful for

A Bible Verse or something positive I will reflect on today is

I feel   very grumpy   grumpy   OK neutral   happy   very happy

because

Jesus Loves Me

Dear God, I love you and want you to know

Something I did well today was

Something important I learned today was

The best part of my day today was

My evening prayer: Tonight I pray

For others, I pray

Final thoughts (Example: forgiveness, special mention, requests)

Date: S   M   T   W   TH   F   S   _____/_____/_____

Dear God, I love you and want you to know

Today will be a great day because

Today I am grateful for

A Bible Verse or something positive I will reflect on today is

I feel   very grumpy   grumpy   OK neutral   happy   very happy

because

Jesus Loves Me

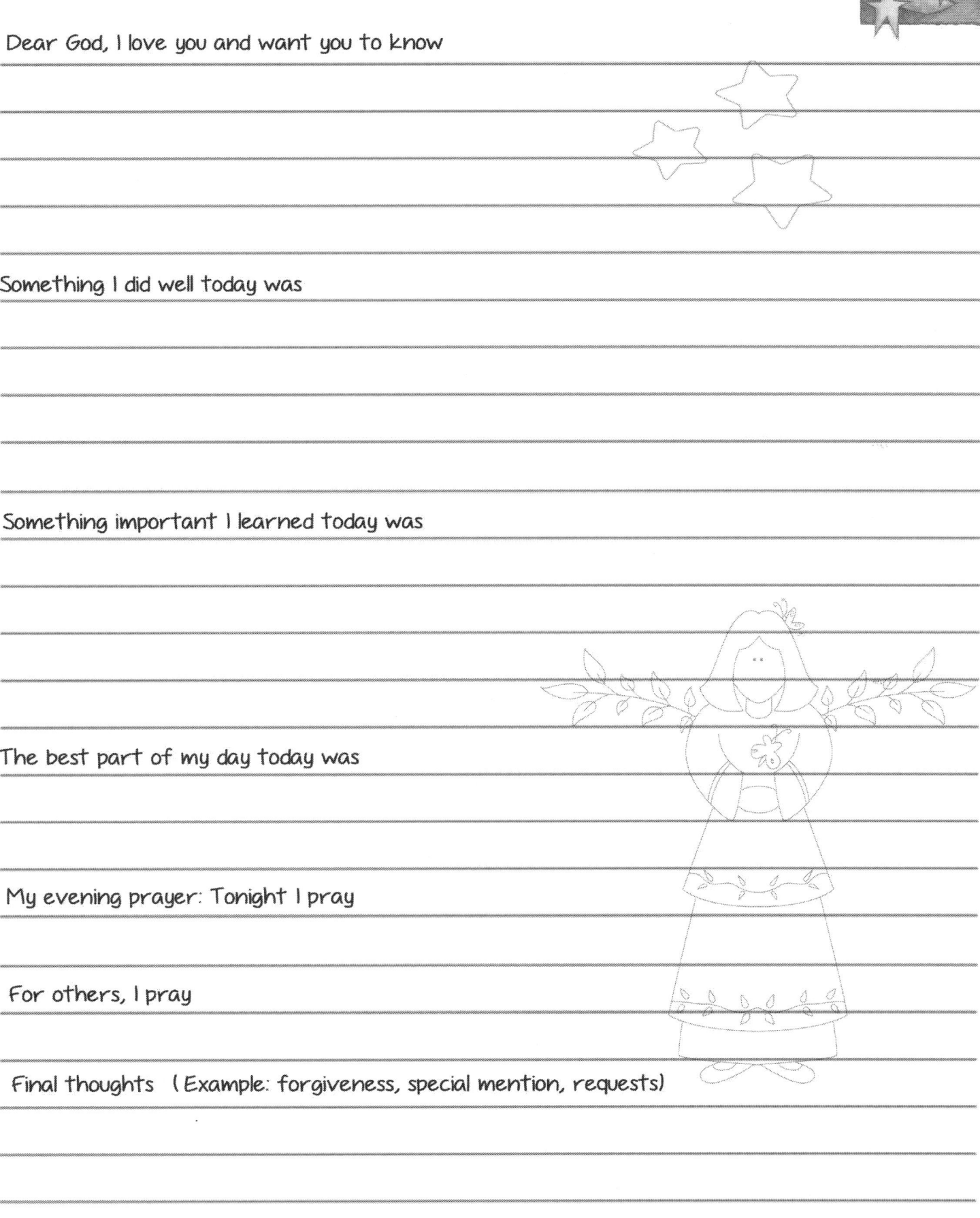

Dear God, I love you and want you to know

_____
_____
_____
_____

Something I did well today was

_____
_____
_____
_____

Something important I learned today was

_____
_____
_____

The best part of my day today was

_____
_____

My evening prayer: Tonight I pray

_____

For others, I pray

_____

Final thoughts (Example: forgiveness, special mention, requests)

_____
_____

Date: S   M   T   W   TH   F   S   _____/_____/_____

Dear God, I love you and want you to know

Today will be a great day because

Today I am grateful for

A Bible Verse or something positive I will reflect on today is

I feel   very grumpy   grumpy   OK neutral   happy   very happy

because

Jesus Loves Me

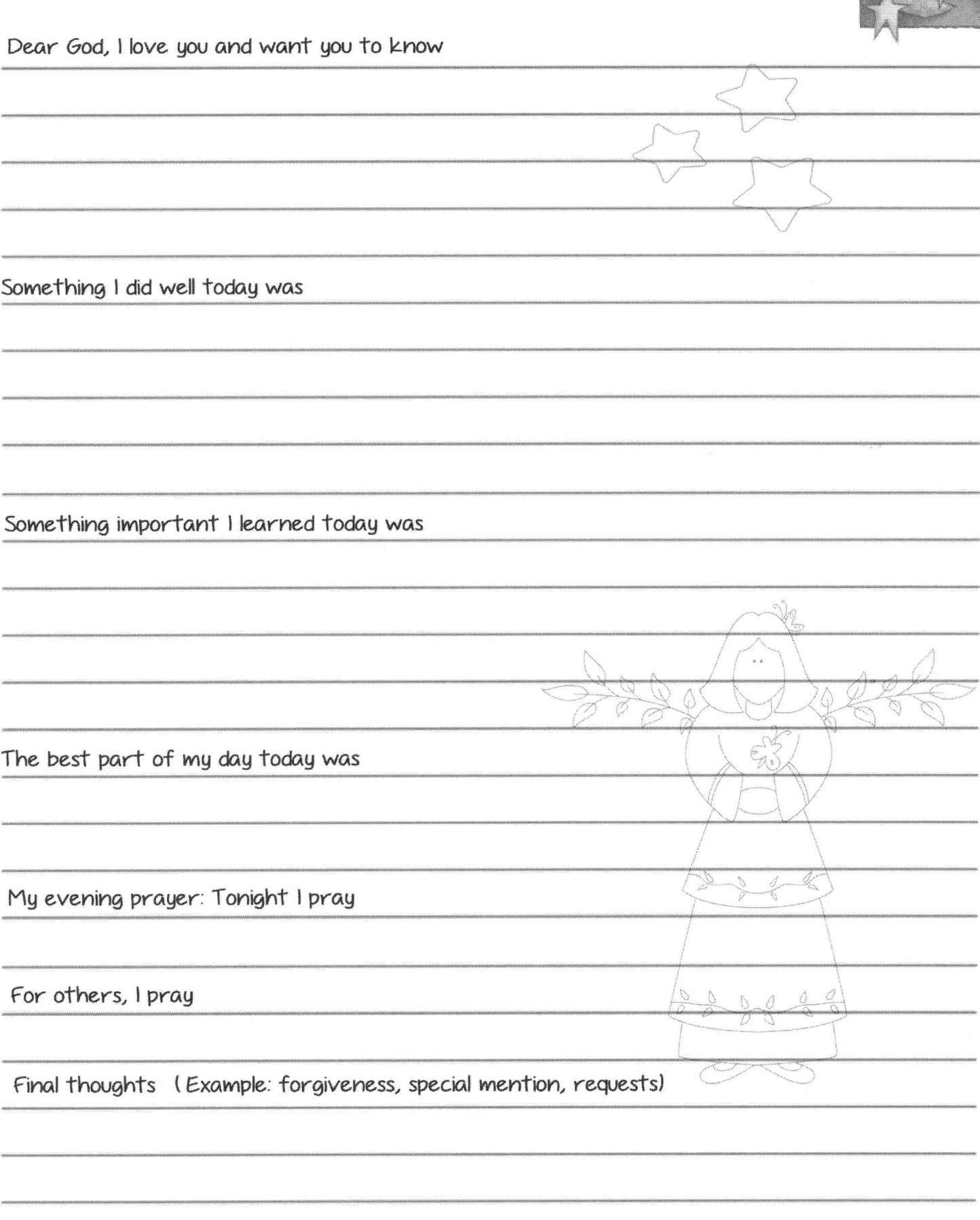

Dear God, I love you and want you to know

Something I did well today was

Something important I learned today was

The best part of my day today was

My evening prayer: Tonight I pray

For others, I pray

Final thoughts (Example: forgiveness, special mention, requests)

Date: S   M   T   W   TH   F   S   _____/_____/_____

Dear God, I love you and want you to know

Today will be a great day because

Today I am grateful for

A Bible Verse or something positive I will reflect on today is

I feel   very grumpy   grumpy   OK neutral   happy   very happy

because

Jesus Loves Me

Dear God, I love you and want you to know

Something I did well today was

Something important I learned today was

The best part of my day today was

My evening prayer: Tonight I pray

For others, I pray

Final thoughts (Example: forgiveness, special mention, requests)

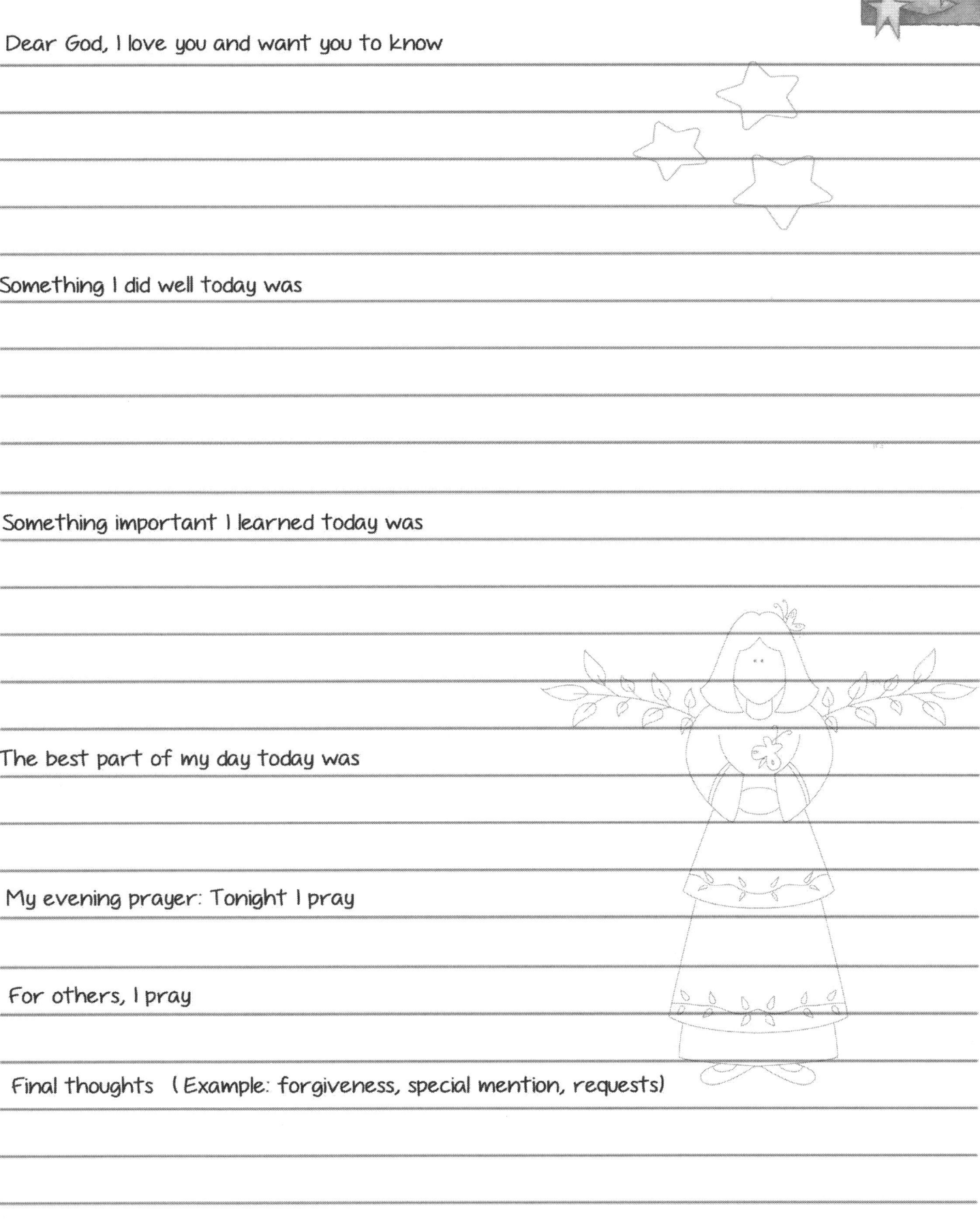

Date: S M T W TH F S _____/_____/_____

Dear God, I love you and want you to know

Today will be a great day because

Today I am grateful for

A Bible Verse or something positive I will reflect on today is

I feel

very grumpy   grumpy   OK neutral   happy   very happy

because

Jesus Loves Me

Dear God, I love you and want you to know

Something I did well today was

Something important I learned today was

The best part of my day today was

My evening prayer: Tonight I pray

For others, I pray

Final thoughts (Example: forgiveness, special mention, requests)

Date: S   M   T   W   TH   F   S   _____/_____/_____

Dear God, I love you and want you to know

Today will be a great day because

Today I am grateful for

A Bible Verse or something positive I will reflect on today is

I feel   very grumpy   grumpy   OK neutral   happy   very happy

because

Jesus Loves Me

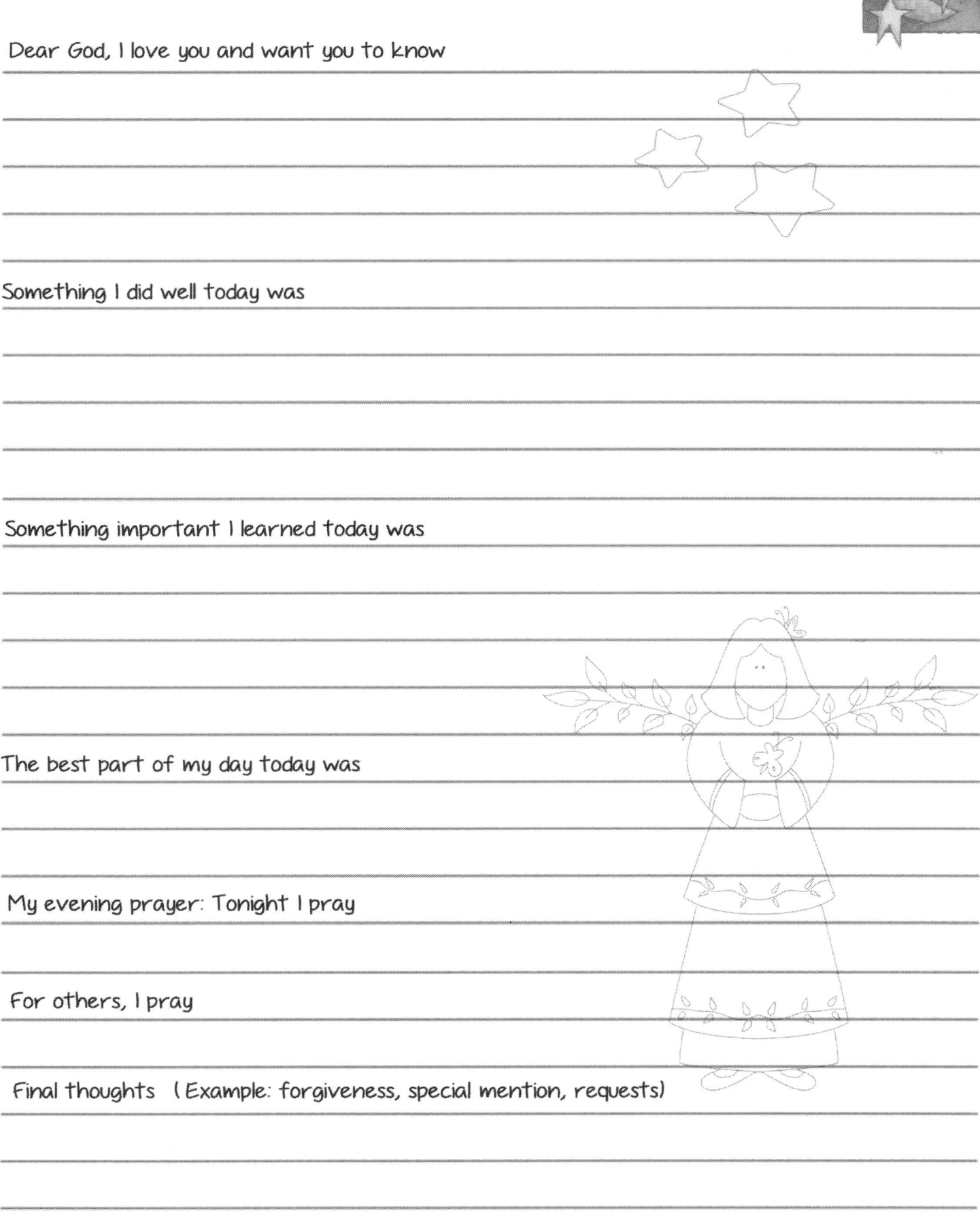

Dear God, I love you and want you to know

Something I did well today was

Something important I learned today was

The best part of my day today was

My evening prayer: Tonight I pray

For others, I pray

Final thoughts (Example: forgiveness, special mention, requests)

Date: S M T W TH F S   _____/_____/_____

Dear God, I love you and want you to know

Today will be a great day because

Today I am grateful for

A Bible Verse or something positive I will reflect on today is

I feel   very grumpy   grumpy   OK neutral   happy   very happy

because

Jesus Loves Me

Dear God, I love you and want you to know

Something I did well today was

Something important I learned today was

The best part of my day today was

My evening prayer: Tonight I pray

For others, I pray

Final thoughts (Example: forgiveness, special mention, requests)

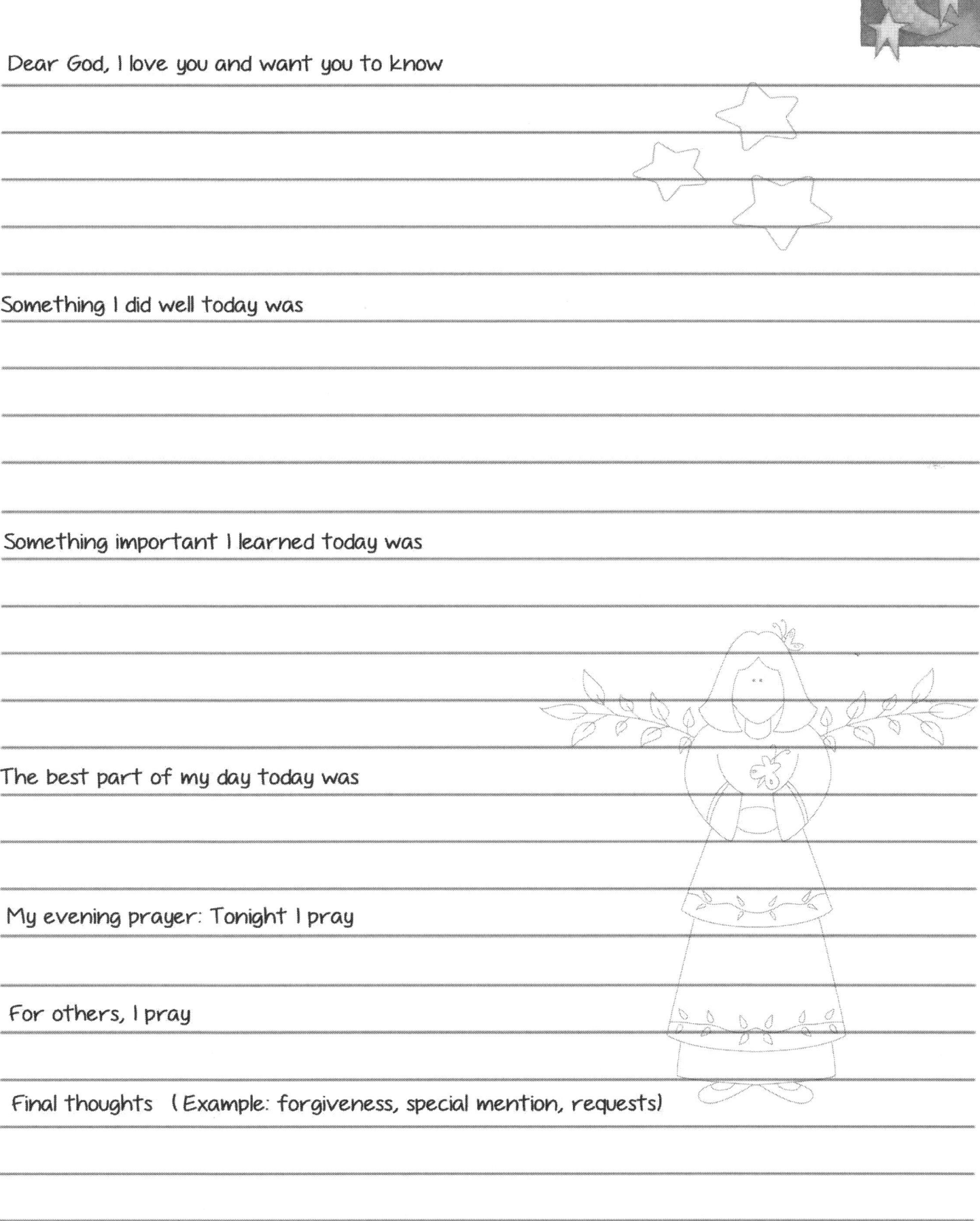

Date: S   M   T   W   TH   F   S   _____/_____/_____

Dear God, I love you and want you to know
_____
_____
_____
_____

Today will be a great day because
_____
_____
_____
_____
_____

Today I am grateful for
_____
_____
_____
_____
_____

A Bible Verse or something positive I will reflect on today is
_____
_____
_____

I feel   very grumpy   grumpy   OK neutral   happy   very happy

because
_____
_____
_____
_____

Jesus Loves Me

Dear God, I love you and want you to know

Something I did well today was

Something important I learned today was

The best part of my day today was

My evening prayer: Tonight I pray

For others, I pray

Final thoughts (Example: forgiveness, special mention, requests)

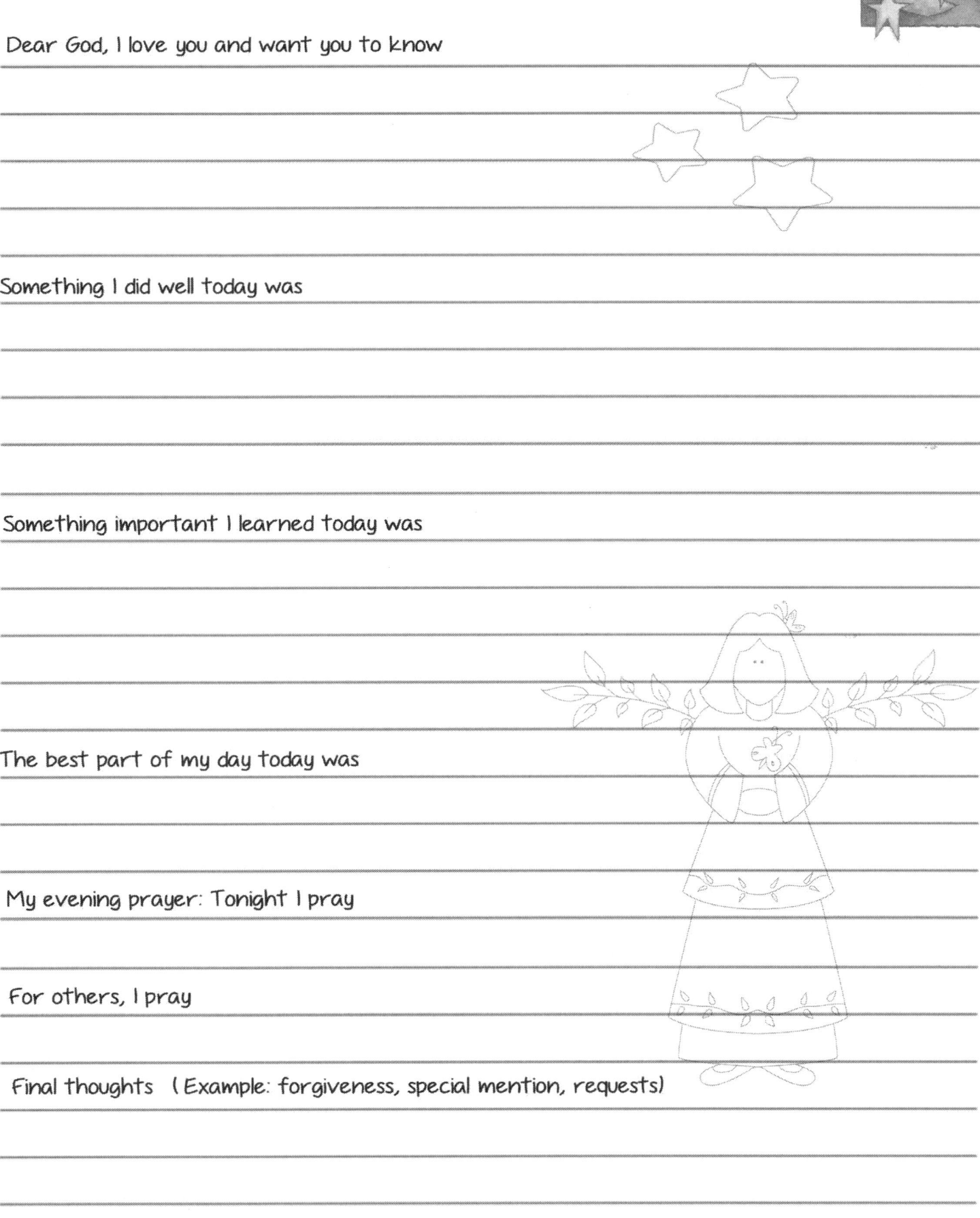

Date: S M T W TH F S _____/_____/_____

Dear God, I love you and want you to know

Today will be a great day because

Today I am grateful for

A Bible Verse or something positive I will reflect on today is

I feel

very grumpy   grumpy   OK neutral   happy   very happy

because

Jesus Loves Me

Dear God, I love you and want you to know

Something I did well today was

Something important I learned today was

The best part of my day today was

My evening prayer: Tonight I pray

For others, I pray

Final thoughts (Example: forgiveness, special mention, requests)

Date: S   M   T   W   TH   F   S   _____/_____/_____

Dear God, I love you and want you to know

_____
_____
_____
_____

Today will be a great day because

_____
_____
_____
_____
_____
_____

Today I am grateful for

_____
_____
_____
_____
_____

A Bible Verse or something positive I will reflect on today is

_____
_____
_____
_____

I feel   very grumpy   grumpy   OK neutral   happy   very happy

because

_____
_____
_____

Jesus Loves Me

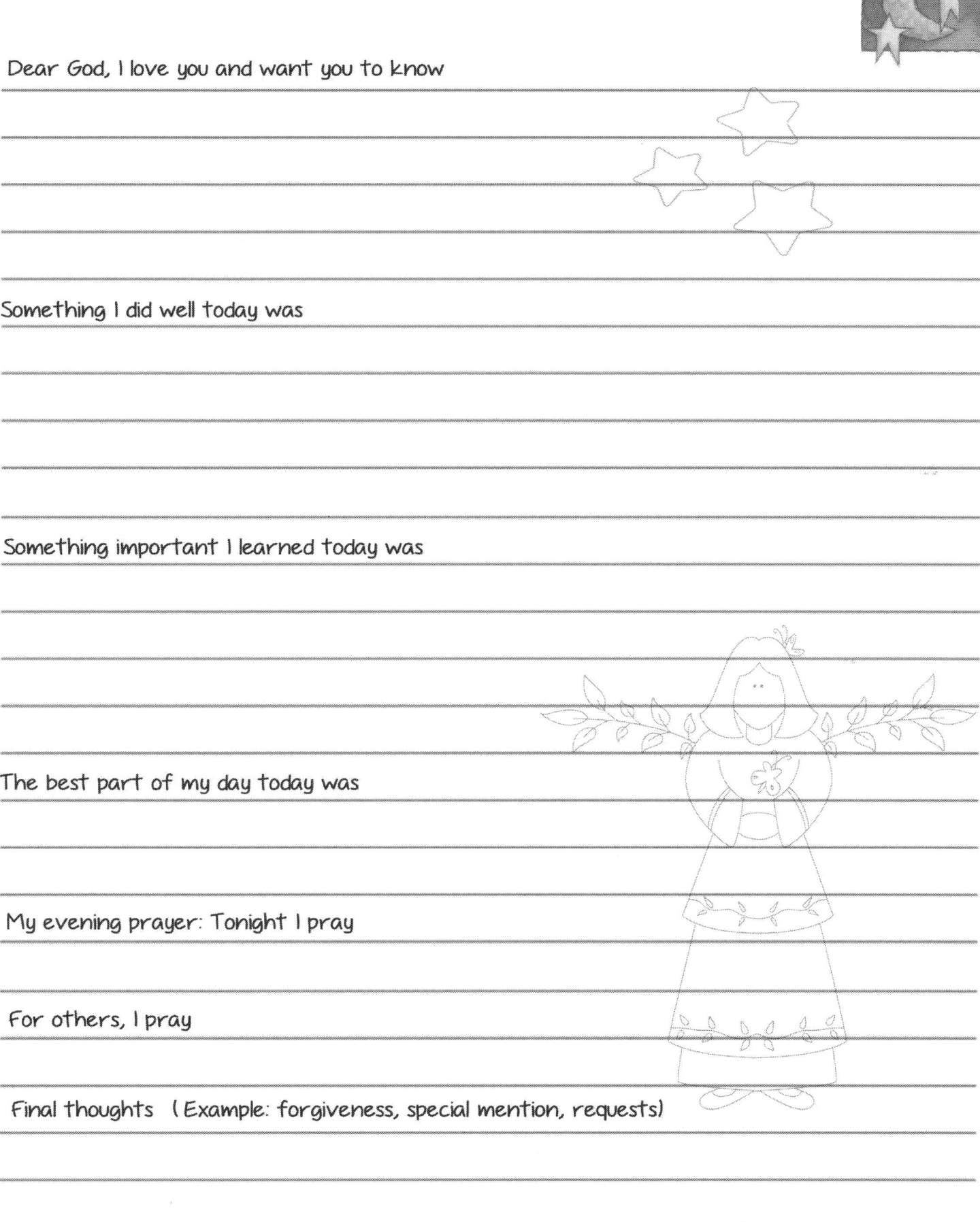

Dear God, I love you and want you to know

Something I did well today was

Something important I learned today was

The best part of my day today was

My evening prayer: Tonight I pray

For others, I pray

Final thoughts (Example: forgiveness, special mention, requests)

Date: S   M   T   W   TH   F   S   _____/_____/_____

Dear God, I love you and want you to know

Today will be a great day because

Today I am grateful for

A Bible Verse or something positive I will reflect on today is

I feel   very grumpy   grumpy   OK neutral   happy   very happy

because

Jesus Loves Me

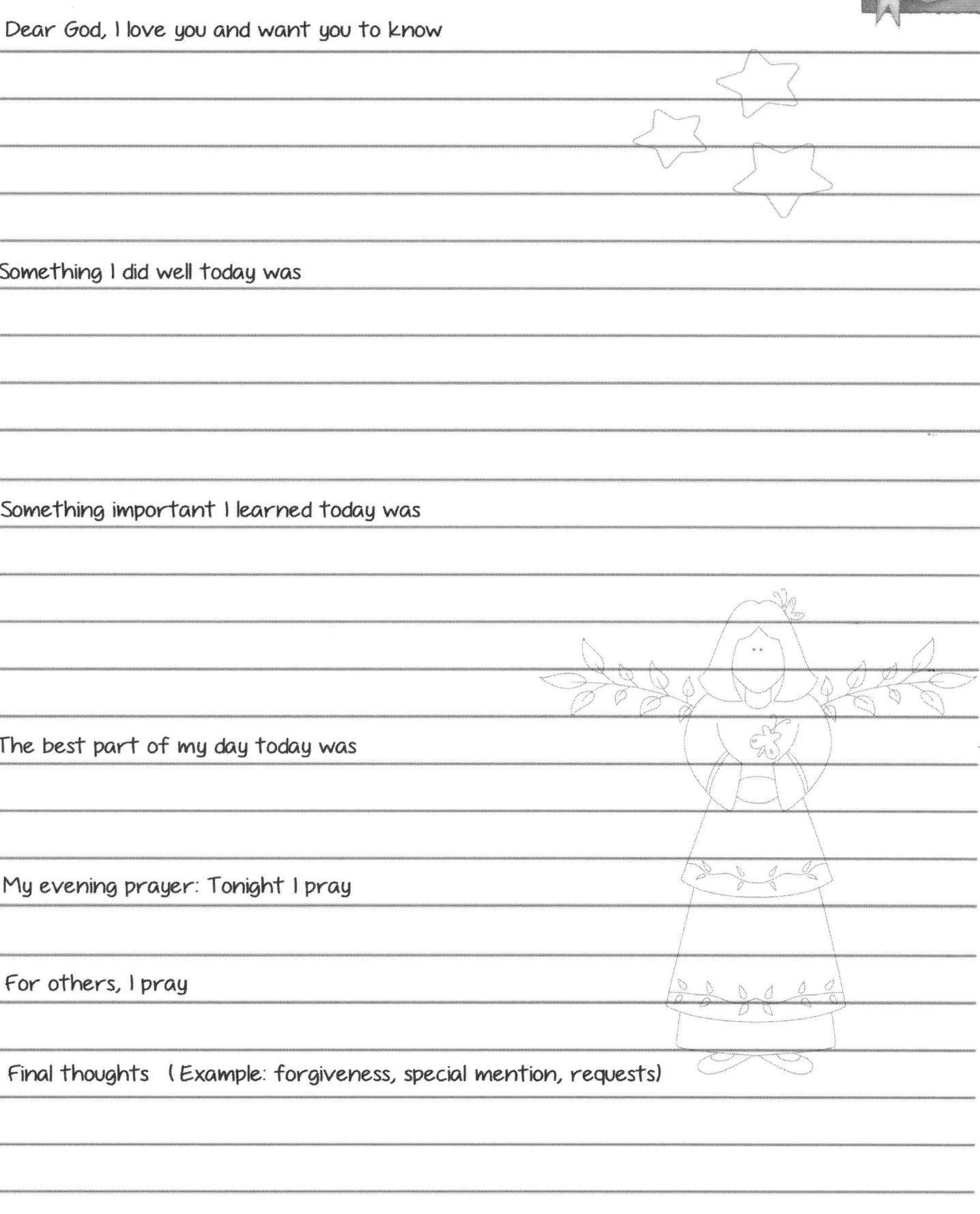

Dear God, I love you and want you to know

Something I did well today was

Something important I learned today was

The best part of my day today was

My evening prayer: Tonight I pray

For others, I pray

Final thoughts (Example: forgiveness, special mention, requests)

Date: S M T W TH F S _____/_____/_____

Dear God, I love you and want you to know

Today will be a great day because

Today I am grateful for

A Bible Verse or something positive I will reflect on today is

I feel   very grumpy   grumpy   OK neutral   happy   very happy

because

Jesus Loves Me

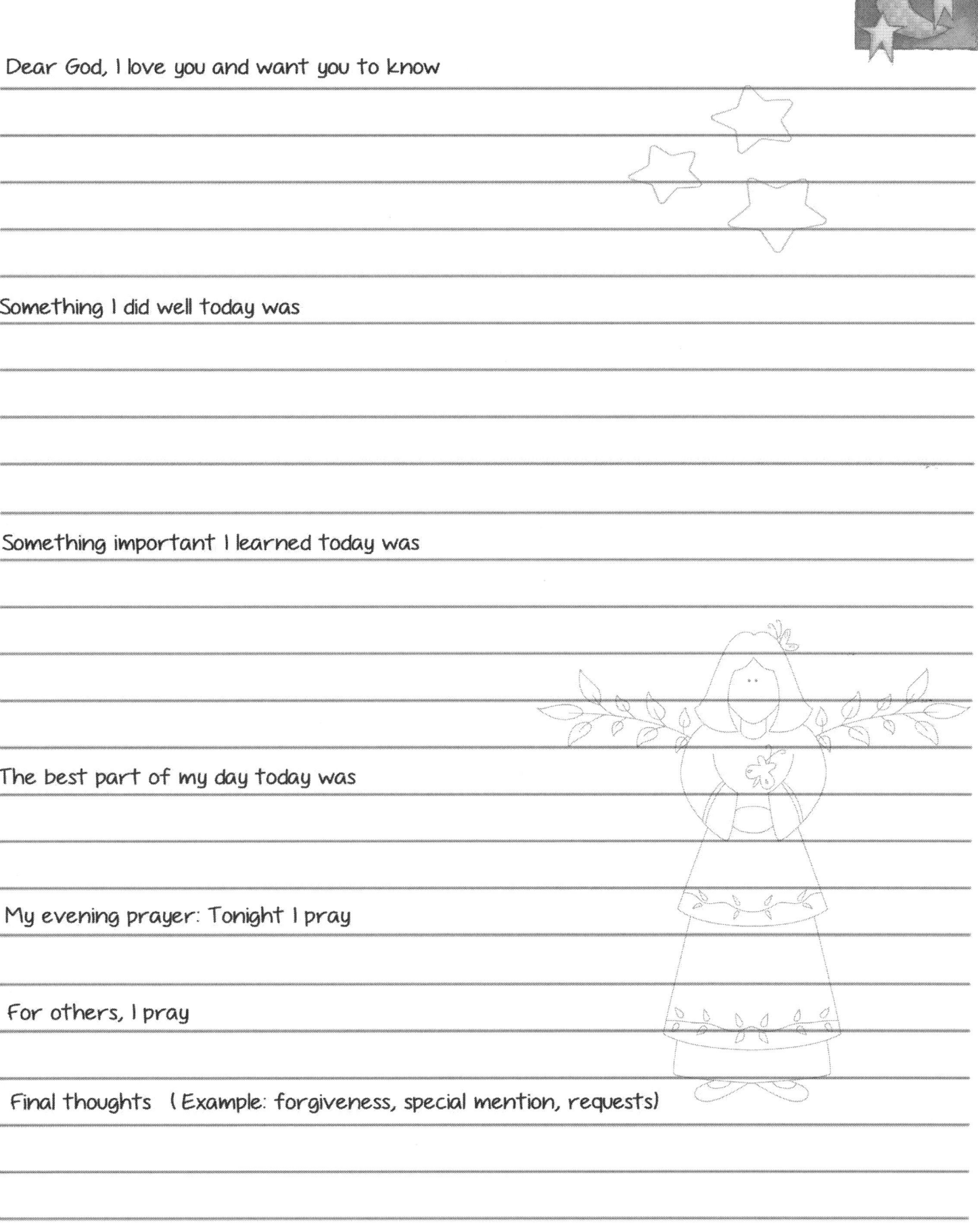

Dear God, I love you and want you to know

Something I did well today was

Something important I learned today was

The best part of my day today was

My evening prayer: Tonight I pray

For others, I pray

Final thoughts (Example: forgiveness, special mention, requests)

Date: S   M   T   W   TH   F   S   _____/_____/_____

Dear God, I love you and want you to know

Today will be a great day because

Today I am grateful for

A Bible Verse or something positive I will reflect on today is

I feel   very grumpy   grumpy   OK neutral   happy   very happy

because

Jesus Loves Me

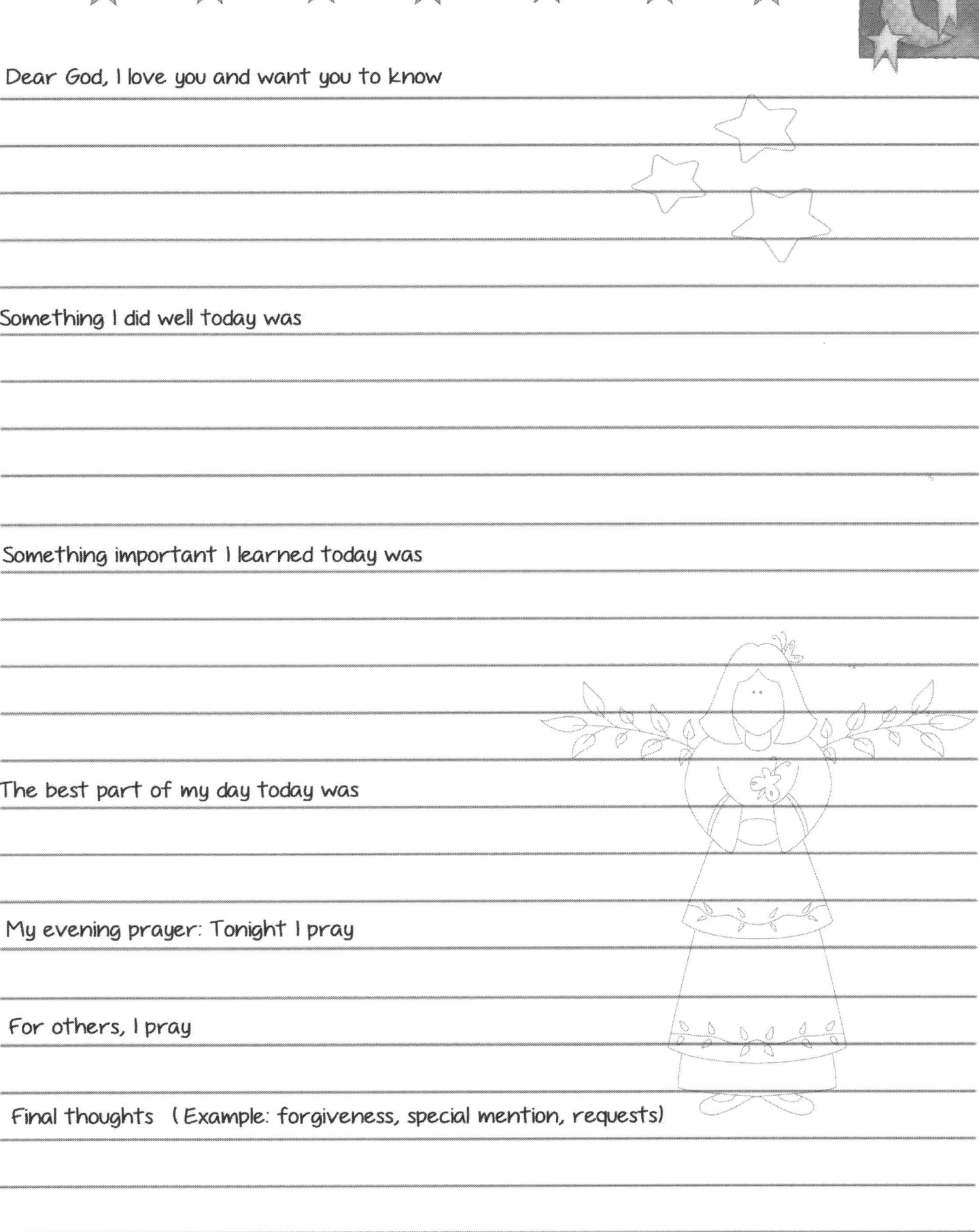

Dear God, I love you and want you to know

Something I did well today was

Something important I learned today was

The best part of my day today was

My evening prayer: Tonight I pray

For others, I pray

Final thoughts (Example: forgiveness, special mention, requests)

Date:　S　M　T　W　TH　F　S　_____/_____/_____

Dear God, I love you and want you to know

Today will be a great day because

Today I am grateful for

A Bible Verse or something positive I will reflect on today is

I feel

very grumpy　　grumpy　　OK neutral　　happy　　very happy

because

Jesus Loves Me

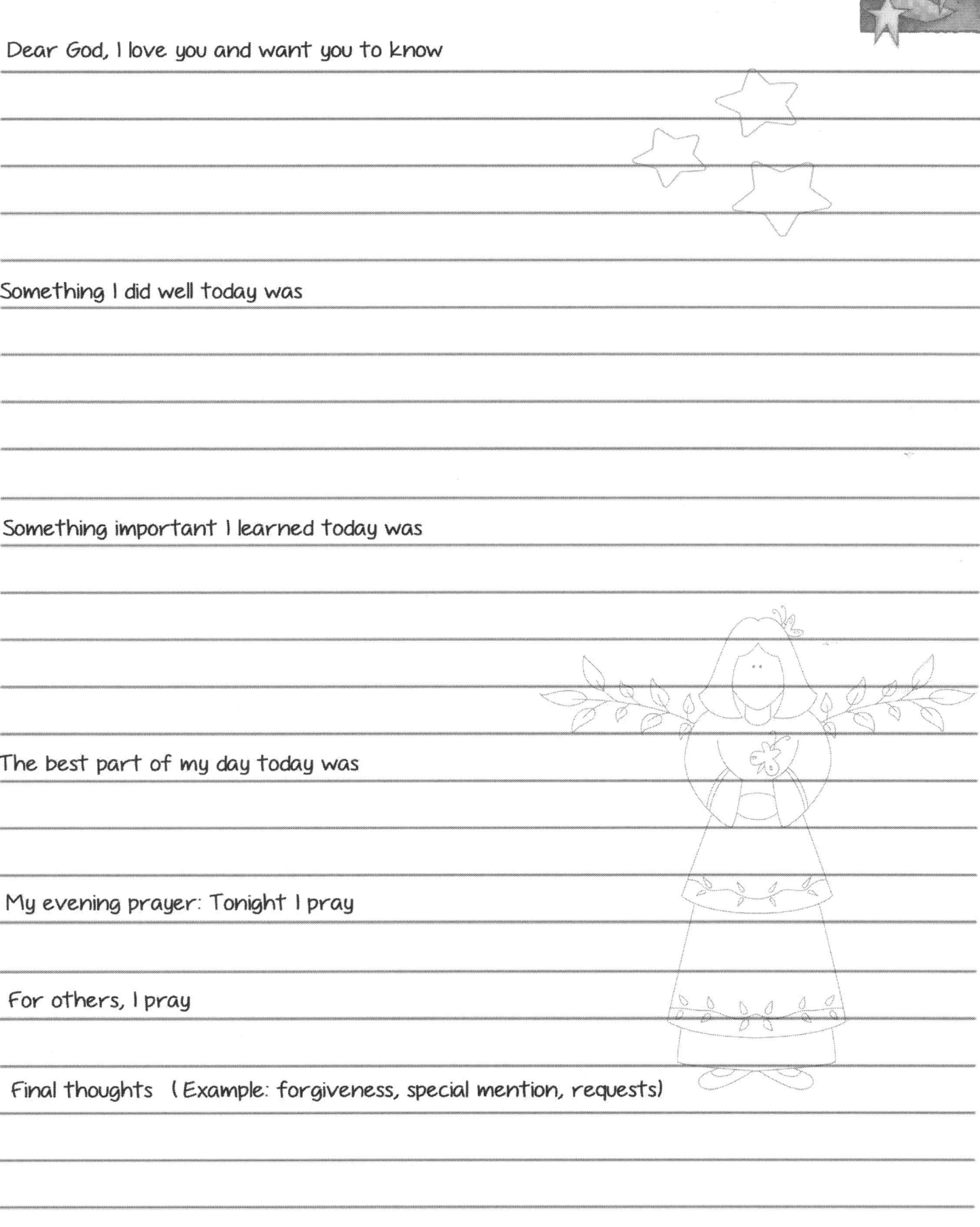

Dear God, I love you and want you to know

Something I did well today was

Something important I learned today was

The best part of my day today was

My evening prayer: Tonight I pray

For others, I pray

Final thoughts (Example: forgiveness, special mention, requests)

Date: S M T W TH F S _____/_____/_____

Dear God, I love you and want you to know
_____
_____
_____
_____

Today will be a great day because
_____
_____
_____
_____

Today I am grateful for
_____
_____
_____
_____

A Bible Verse or something positive I will reflect on today is
_____
_____
_____

I feel   very grumpy   grumpy   OK neutral   happy   very happy

because
_____
_____
_____

Jesus Loves Me

Dear God, I love you and want you to know

Something I did well today was

Something important I learned today was

The best part of my day today was

My evening prayer: Tonight I pray

For others, I pray

Final thoughts (Example: forgiveness, special mention, requests)

Date: S M T W TH F S _____/_____/_____

Dear God, I love you and want you to know
_____
_____
_____
_____

Today will be a great day because
_____
_____
_____
_____

Today I am grateful for
_____
_____
_____
_____

A Bible Verse or something positive I will reflect on today is
_____
_____
_____

I feel   very grumpy   grumpy   OK neutral   happy   very happy

because
_____
_____
_____

Jesus Loves Me

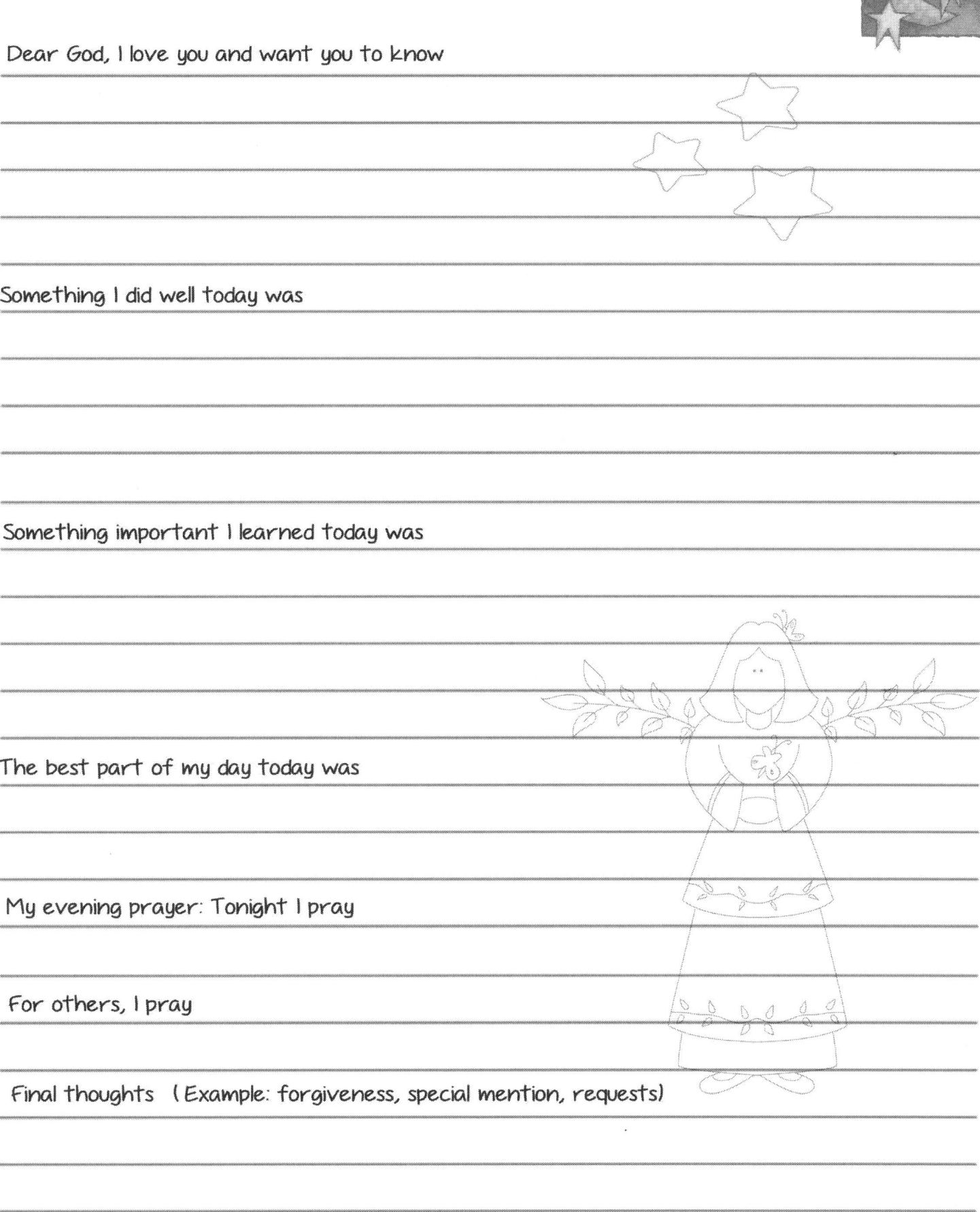

Dear God, I love you and want you to know

Something I did well today was

Something important I learned today was

The best part of my day today was

My evening prayer: Tonight I pray

For others, I pray

Final thoughts   (Example: forgiveness, special mention, requests)

Date: S M T W TH F S _____/_____/_____

Dear God, I love you and want you to know

_____
_____
_____

Today will be a great day because

_____
_____
_____
_____
_____

Today I am grateful for

_____
_____
_____
_____

A Bible Verse or something positive I will reflect on today is

_____
_____
_____

I feel   very grumpy   grumpy   OK neutral   happy   very happy

because

_____
_____
_____

Jesus Loves Me

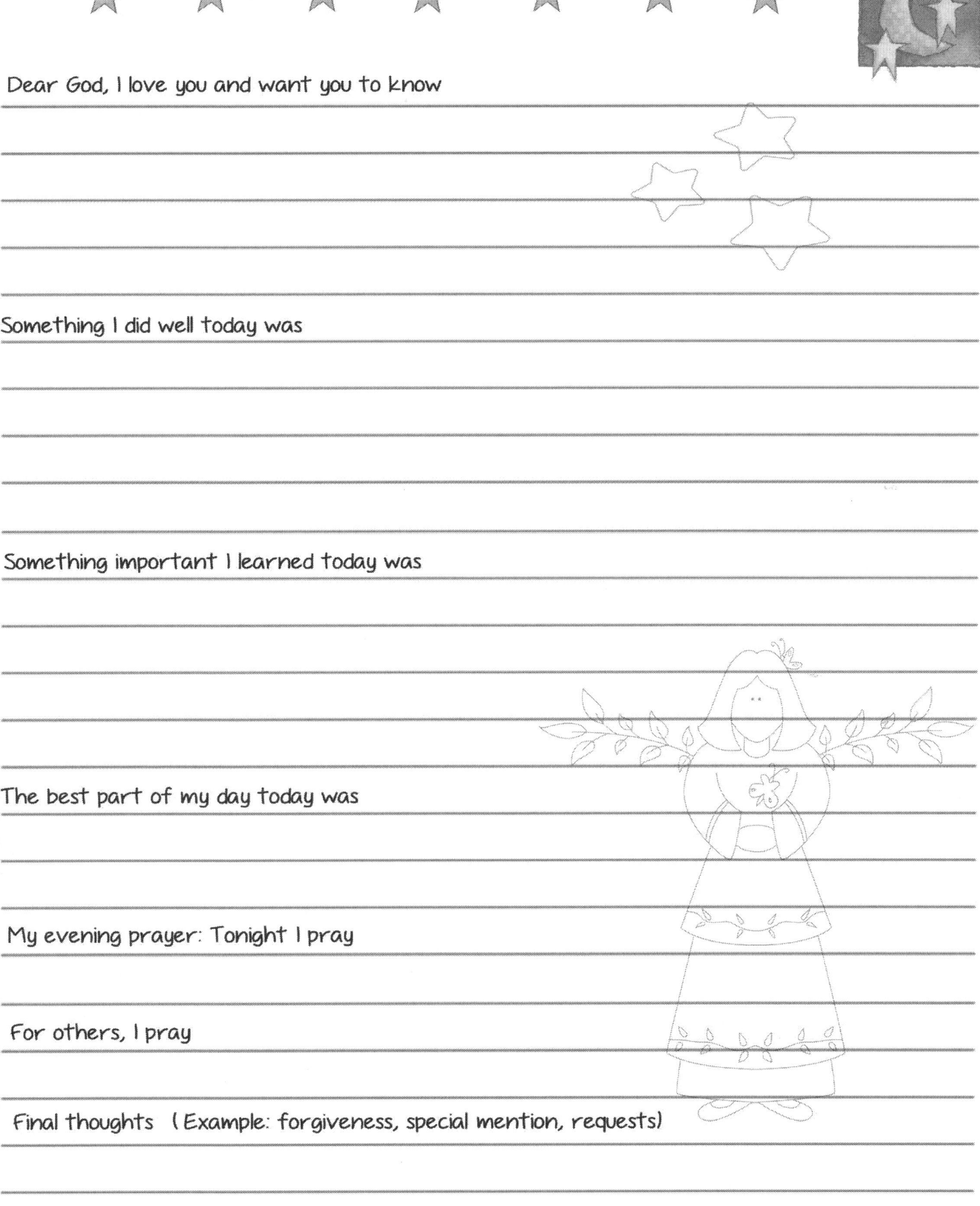

Dear God, I love you and want you to know

Something I did well today was

Something important I learned today was

The best part of my day today was

My evening prayer: Tonight I pray

For others, I pray

Final thoughts (Example: forgiveness, special mention, requests)

Date: S   M   T   W   TH   F   S   _____/_____/_____

Dear God, I love you and want you to know
_____
_____
_____
_____

Today will be a great day because
_____
_____
_____
_____

Today I am grateful for
_____
_____
_____
_____

A Bible Verse or something positive I will reflect on today is
_____
_____
_____

I feel   😢   😐   😶   🙂   😊
        very grumpy   grumpy   OK neutral   happy   very happy
because
_____
_____
_____

Jesus Loves Me

Dear God, I love you and want you to know

Something I did well today was

Something important I learned today was

The best part of my day today was

My evening prayer: Tonight I pray

For others, I pray

Final thoughts (Example: forgiveness, special mention, requests)

Date: S M T W TH F S _____/_____/_____

Dear God, I love you and want you to know

Today will be a great day because

Today I am grateful for

A Bible Verse or something positive I will reflect on today is

I feel   very grumpy   grumpy   OK neutral   happy   very happy

because

Jesus Loves Me

Dear God, I love you and want you to know

Something I did well today was

Something important I learned today was

The best part of my day today was

My evening prayer: Tonight I pray

For others, I pray

Final thoughts (Example: forgiveness, special mention, requests)

Date: S   M   T   W   TH   F   S   _____/_____/_____

Dear God, I love you and want you to know

Today will be a great day because

Today I am grateful for

A Bible Verse or something positive I will reflect on today is

I feel

because

very grumpy   grumpy   OK neutral   happy   very happy

Jesus Loves Me

Dear God, I love you and want you to know

Something I did well today was

Something important I learned today was

The best part of my day today was

My evening prayer: Tonight I pray

For others, I pray

Final thoughts   (Example: forgiveness, special mention, requests)

Date: S   M   T   W   TH   F   S   _____/_____/_____

Dear God, I love you and want you to know

Today will be a great day because

Today I am grateful for

A Bible Verse or something positive I will reflect on today is

I feel   very grumpy   grumpy   OK neutral   happy   very happy

because

Jesus Loves Me

Dear God, I love you and want you to know

Something I did well today was

Something important I learned today was

The best part of my day today was

My evening prayer: Tonight I pray

For others, I pray

Final thoughts (Example: forgiveness, special mention, requests)

Date: S   M   T   W   TH   F   S   _____ / _____ / _____

Dear God, I love you and want you to know

Today will be a great day because

Today I am grateful for

A Bible Verse or something positive I will reflect on today is

I feel   very grumpy   grumpy   OK neutral   happy   very happy

because

Jesus Loves Me

Dear God, I love you and want you to know

Something I did well today was

Something important I learned today was

The best part of my day today was

My evening prayer: Tonight I pray

For others, I pray

Final thoughts (Example: forgiveness, special mention, requests)

Date: S M T W TH F S   _____/_____/_____

Dear God, I love you and want you to know

Today will be a great day because

Today I am grateful for

A Bible Verse or something positive I will reflect on today is

I feel   very grumpy   grumpy   OK neutral   happy   very happy

because

Jesus Loves Me

Dear God, I love you and want you to know

Something I did well today was

Something important I learned today was

The best part of my day today was

My evening prayer: Tonight I pray

For others, I pray

Final thoughts (Example: forgiveness, special mention, requests)

Date: S   M   T   W   TH   F   S   _____/_____/_____

Dear God, I love you and want you to know

Today will be a great day because

Today I am grateful for

A Bible Verse or something positive I will reflect on today is

I feel   very grumpy   grumpy   OK neutral   happy   very happy

because

Jesus Loves Me

Dear God, I love you and want you to know

Something I did well today was

Something important I learned today was

The best part of my day today was

My evening prayer: Tonight I pray

For others, I pray

Final thoughts (Example: forgiveness, special mention, requests)

Date: S M T W TH F S _____/_____/_____

Dear God, I love you and want you to know

Today will be a great day because

Today I am grateful for

A Bible Verse or something positive I will reflect on today is

I feel

very grumpy   grumpy   OK neutral   happy   very happy

because

Jesus Loves Me

Dear God, I love you and want you to know

Something I did well today was

Something important I learned today was

The best part of my day today was

My evening prayer: Tonight I pray

For others, I pray

Final thoughts (Example: forgiveness, special mention, requests)

Date: S   M   T   W   TH   F   S   _____/_____/_____

Dear God, I love you and want you to know

Today will be a great day because

Today I am grateful for

A Bible Verse or something positive I will reflect on today is

I feel   very grumpy   grumpy   OK neutral   happy   very happy

because

Jesus Loves Me

Dear God, I love you and want you to know

Something I did well today was

Something important I learned today was

The best part of my day today was

My evening prayer: Tonight I pray

For others, I pray

Final thoughts (Example: forgiveness, special mention, requests)

Date: S M T W TH F S _____/_____/_____

Dear God, I love you and want you to know

Today will be a great day because

Today I am grateful for

A Bible Verse or something positive I will reflect on today is

I feel

very grumpy   grumpy   OK neutral   happy   very happy

because

Jesus Loves Me

Dear God, I love you and want you to know

Something I did well today was

Something important I learned today was

The best part of my day today was

My evening prayer: Tonight I pray

For others, I pray

Final thoughts (Example: forgiveness, special mention, requests)

Date: S   M   T   W   TH   F   S   _____/_____/_____

Dear God, I love you and want you to know

Today will be a great day because

Today I am grateful for

A Bible Verse or something positive I will reflect on today is

I feel   very grumpy   grumpy   OK neutral   happy   very happy

because

Jesus Loves Me

Dear God, I love you and want you to know

Something I did well today was

Something important I learned today was

The best part of my day today was

My evening prayer: Tonight I pray

For others, I pray

Final thoughts (Example: forgiveness, special mention, requests)

Date: S M T W TH F S _____/_____/_____

Dear God, I love you and want you to know

_____
_____
_____
_____

Today will be a great day because

_____
_____
_____
_____
_____

Today I am grateful for

_____
_____
_____
_____
_____

A Bible Verse or something positive I will reflect on today is

_____
_____
_____

I feel

    very grumpy   grumpy   OK neutral   happy   very happy

because _____
_____
_____
_____

Jesus Loves Me

Dear God, I love you and want you to know

Something I did well today was

Something important I learned today was

The best part of my day today was

My evening prayer: Tonight I pray

For others, I pray

Final thoughts (Example: forgiveness, special mention, requests)

Date: S   M   T   W   TH   F   S   _____/_____/_____

Dear God, I love you and want you to know

Today will be a great day because

Today I am grateful for

A Bible Verse or something positive I will reflect on today is

I feel

very grumpy   grumpy   OK neutral   happy   very happy

because

Jesus Loves Me

Dear God, I love you and want you to know

Something I did well today was

Something important I learned today was

The best part of my day today was

My evening prayer: Tonight I pray

For others, I pray

Final thoughts (Example: forgiveness, special mention, requests)

Date: S   M   T   W   TH   F   S   _____/_____/_____

Dear God, I love you and want you to know

_____
_____
_____
_____

Today will be a great day because

_____
_____
_____
_____

Today I am grateful for

_____
_____
_____
_____

A Bible Verse or something positive I will reflect on today is

_____
_____
_____

I feel   very grumpy   grumpy   OK neutral   happy   very happy

because
_____
_____
_____

Jesus Loves Me

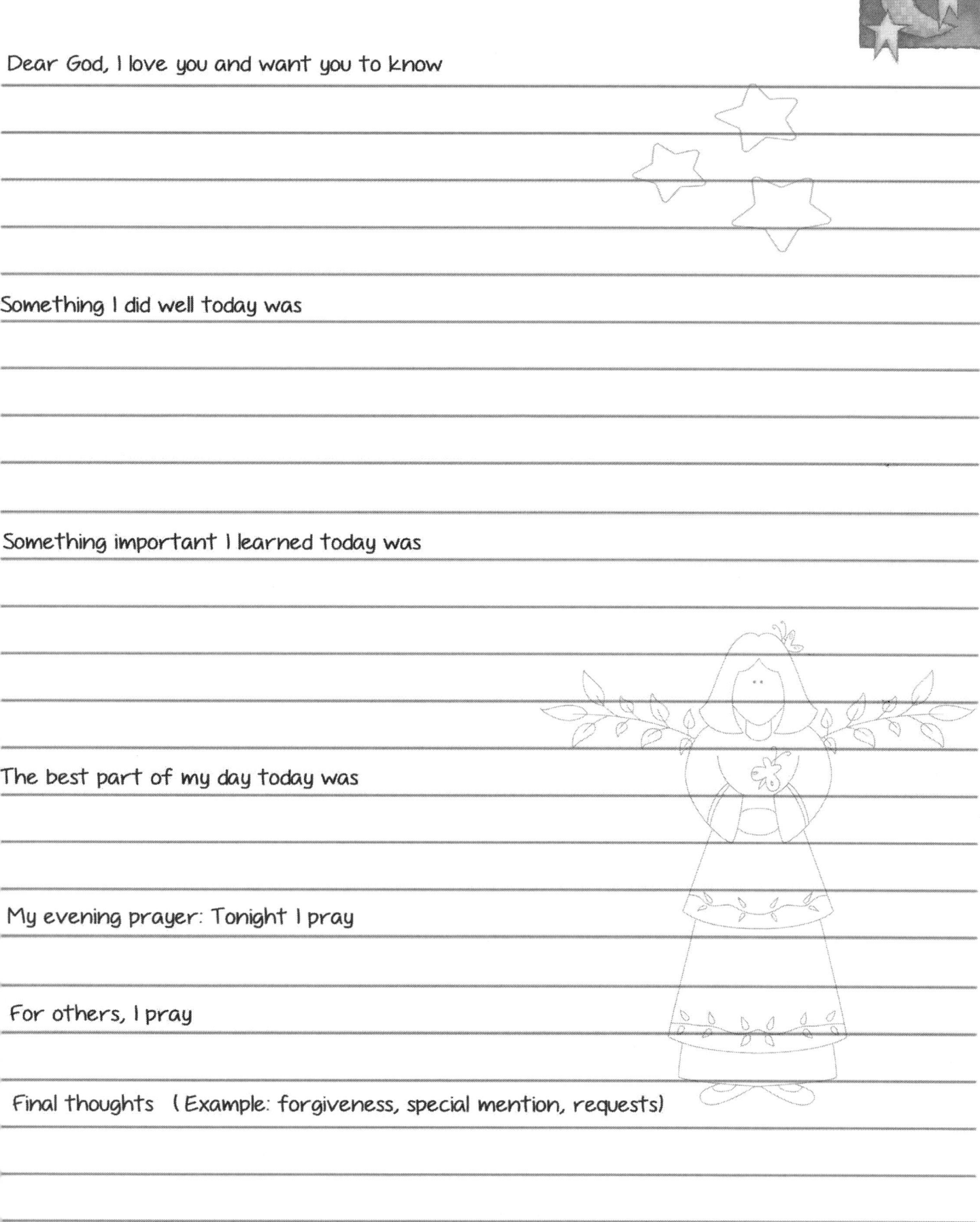

Dear God, I love you and want you to know

Something I did well today was

Something important I learned today was

The best part of my day today was

My evening prayer: Tonight I pray

For others, I pray

Final thoughts (Example: forgiveness, special mention, requests)

Date: S   M   T   W   TH   F   S   _____/_____/_____

Dear God, I love you and want you to know
_____
_____
_____

Today will be a great day because
_____
_____
_____
_____

Today I am grateful for
_____
_____
_____
_____

A Bible Verse or something positive I will reflect on today is
_____
_____
_____

I feel   very grumpy   grumpy   OK neutral   happy   very happy

because
_____
_____
_____

Jesus Loves Me

Dear God, I love you and want you to know

Something I did well today was

Something important I learned today was

The best part of my day today was

My evening prayer: Tonight I pray

For others, I pray

Final thoughts   (Example: forgiveness, special mention, requests)

Date: S   M   T   W   TH   F   S   _____/_____/_____

Dear God, I love you and want you to know

Today will be a great day because

Today I am grateful for

A Bible Verse or something positive I will reflect on today is

I feel   very grumpy   grumpy   OK neutral   happy   very happy

because

Jesus Loves Me

Dear God, I love you and want you to know

Something I did well today was

Something important I learned today was

The best part of my day today was

My evening prayer: Tonight I pray

For others, I pray

Final thoughts (Example: forgiveness, special mention, requests)

Date: S   M   T   W   TH   F   S   _____/_____/_____

Dear God, I love you and want you to know

Today will be a great day because

Today I am grateful for

A Bible Verse or something positive I will reflect on today is

I feel   very grumpy   grumpy   OK neutral   happy   very happy

because

Jesus Loves Me

Dear God, I love you and want you to know

Something I did well today was

Something important I learned today was

The best part of my day today was

My evening prayer: Tonight I pray

For others, I pray

Final thoughts (Example: forgiveness, special mention, requests)

Date: S   M   T   W   TH   F   S   _____/_____/_____

Dear God, I love you and want you to know

Today will be a great day because

Today I am grateful for

A Bible Verse or something positive I will reflect on today is

I feel   very grumpy   grumpy   OK neutral   happy   very happy
because

Jesus Loves Me

Dear God, I love you and want you to know

Something I did well today was

Something important I learned today was

The best part of my day today was

My evening prayer: Tonight I pray

For others, I pray

Final thoughts (Example: forgiveness, special mention, requests)

Date: S   M   T   W   TH   F   S   _____/_____/_____

Dear God, I love you and want you to know

Today will be a great day because

Today I am grateful for

A Bible Verse or something positive I will reflect on today is

I feel   very grumpy   grumpy   OK neutral   happy   very happy

because

Jesus Loves Me

Dear God, I love you and want you to know

Something I did well today was

Something important I learned today was

The best part of my day today was

My evening prayer: Tonight I pray

For others, I pray

Final thoughts (Example: forgiveness, special mention, requests)

Date: S   M   T   W   TH   F   S   _____/_____/_____

Dear God, I love you and want you to know

Today will be a great day because

Today I am grateful for

A Bible Verse or something positive I will reflect on today is

I feel

very grumpy   grumpy   OK neutral   happy   very happy

because

Jesus Loves Me

Dear God, I love you and want you to know

Something I did well today was

Something important I learned today was

The best part of my day today was

My evening prayer: Tonight I pray

For others, I pray

Final thoughts (Example: forgiveness, special mention, requests)

Date: S   M   T   W   TH   F   S   _____/_____/_____

Dear God, I love you and want you to know

Today will be a great day because

Today I am grateful for

A Bible Verse or something positive I will reflect on today is

I feel

very grumpy   grumpy   OK neutral   happy   very happy

because

Jesus Loves Me

Dear God, I love you and want you to know

Something I did well today was

Something important I learned today was

The best part of my day today was

My evening prayer: Tonight I pray

For others, I pray

Final thoughts (Example: forgiveness, special mention, requests)

Date: S   M   T   W   TH   F   S   _____/_____/_____

Dear God, I love you and want you to know

Today will be a great day because

Today I am grateful for

A Bible Verse or something positive I will reflect on today is

I feel

            very grumpy   grumpy   OK neutral   happy   very happy

because

Jesus Loves Me

Dear God, I love you and want you to know

Something I did well today was

Something important I learned today was

The best part of my day today was

My evening prayer: Tonight I pray

For others, I pray

Final thoughts (Example: forgiveness, special mention, requests)

Date: S   M   T   W   TH   F   S   _____/_____/_____

Dear God, I love you and want you to know

Today will be a great day because

Today I am grateful for

A Bible Verse or something positive I will reflect on today is

I feel   very grumpy   grumpy   OK neutral   happy   very happy

because

Jesus Loves Me

Dear God, I love you and want you to know

Something I did well today was

Something important I learned today was

The best part of my day today was

My evening prayer: Tonight I pray

For others, I pray

Final thoughts (Example: forgiveness, special mention, requests)

Date: S   M   T   W   TH   F   S   _____/_____/_____

Dear God, I love you and want you to know

Today will be a great day because

Today I am grateful for

A Bible Verse or something positive I will reflect on today is

I feel   very grumpy   grumpy   OK neutral   happy   very happy

because

Jesus Loves Me

Dear God, I love you and want you to know

Something I did well today was

Something important I learned today was

The best part of my day today was

My evening prayer: Tonight I pray

For others, I pray

Final thoughts (Example: forgiveness, special mention, requests)

Date: S   M   T   W   TH   F   S   _____/_____/_____

Dear God, I love you and want you to know

Today will be a great day because

Today I am grateful for

A Bible Verse or something positive I will reflect on today is

I feel   very grumpy   grumpy   OK neutral   happy   very happy

because

Jesus Loves Me

Dear God, I love you and want you to know

Something I did well today was

Something important I learned today was

The best part of my day today was

My evening prayer: Tonight I pray

For others, I pray

Final thoughts (Example: forgiveness, special mention, requests)

Notes

Notes

Notes

Notes

Notes

Notes

Notes

Printed in Great Britain
by Amazon